## Help Me **Understand**

# What Happens When My **Parents** Get Divorced?

**Marisa Orgullo**

**PowerKiDS**
press.

NEW YORK

Published in 2019 by The Rosen Publishing Group, Inc.
29 East 21st Street, New York, NY 10010

First Edition

Editor: Elizabeth Krajnik
Book Design: Rachel Rising

Photo Credits: Cover VGstockstudio/Shutterstock.com; p. 5 ESB Professional/Shutterstock.com; p. 6 Kostikova Natalia/Shutterstock.com; p. 7 OLJ Studio/Shutterstock.com; p. 9 Monkey Business Images/Shutterstock.com; p. 10 Mega Pixel/Shutterstock.com; p. 11 Refat/Shutterstock.com; p. 12 Julia Kuznetsova/Shutterstock.com; p. 13 Andrey_Popov/Shutterstock.com; p. 15 LightField Studios/Shutterstock.com; p. 16 pink_cotton_candy/iStockphoto.com; p.17 Potstock/Shutterstock.com; p. 19 Photographee.eu/Shutterstock.com; p. 21 wavebreakmedia/Shutterstock.com; p. 22 kurhan/Shutterstock.com.


Cataloging-in-Publication Data

Names: Orgullo, Marisa.
Title: What happens when my parents get divorced? / Marisa Orgullo.
Description: New York : PowerKids Press, 2019. | Series: Help me understand | Includes glossary and index.
Identifiers: LCCN ISBN 9781508167129 (pbk.) | ISBN 9781508167105 (library bound) | ISBN 9781508167136 (6 pack)
Subjects: LCSH: Children of divorced parents–Juvenile literature. | Divorce–Juvenile literature.
Classification: LCC HQ777.5 O74 2019 | DDC 306.89–dc23

Manufactured in the United States of America

CPSIA Compliance Information: Batch #CS18PK: For Further Information contact Rosen Publishing, New York, New York at 1-800-237-9932

# Contents

Ending a Marriage . . . . . . . . . . . . . . . . . . . . . . . . . . . . . 4

In the Beginning . . . . . . . . . . . . . . . . . . . . . . . . . . . . . 6

Who Will You Live With? . . . . . . . . . . . . . . . . . . . . . . 8

Splitting Time . . . . . . . . . . . . . . . . . . . . . . . . . . . . . . 10

Long Distance . . . . . . . . . . . . . . . . . . . . . . . . . . . . . 12

Changes for Everyone . . . . . . . . . . . . . . . . . . . . . . 14

Making Things Worse . . . . . . . . . . . . . . . . . . . . . . . 16

How Do You Feel? . . . . . . . . . . . . . . . . . . . . . . . . . . 18

New People . . . . . . . . . . . . . . . . . . . . . . . . . . . . . . . 20

Everything Will Be OK . . . . . . . . . . . . . . . . . . . . . . 22

Glossary . . . . . . . . . . . . . . . . . . . . . . . . . . . . . . . . . . 23

Index . . . . . . . . . . . . . . . . . . . . . . . . . . . . . . . . . . . . 24

Websites . . . . . . . . . . . . . . . . . . . . . . . . . . . . . . . . . 24

# Ending a Marriage

Sometimes parents don't get along or don't feel the same way they felt about each other when they first got married. Some parents often argue. As a result, some people choose to get divorced.

A divorce is when two people end their marriage in the eyes of the law. Whatever reason your parents have for getting divorced, it's not your fault. Getting divorced doesn't mean that your parents don't love you. Many times, parents get divorced because they think it's better for their children in the long run.

Getting a divorce might be what's best for your parents. If they often fight around you, that's not good.

# In the Beginning

When your parents were younger, they might have spent a lot of time together. Then they decided they wanted to get married and spend the rest of their lives together. They started a family and had you.

At some point, things changed between your parents. Maybe one parent fell in love with someone else or perhaps they formed habits that the other parent didn't like. Divorces don't come out of nowhere. Your parents may have felt at odds for quite a while.

Over time, your parents probably did things together less and less. They may have stopped spending time with each other entirely.

7

# Who Will You Live With?

In most cases, when parents get divorced they move into separate houses or apartments. Your parents will have to work together to decide who will have **custody** of you and your brothers or sisters. This might mean they have to hire a **lawyer**. Some parents can reach a decision without a lawyer, though.

Your parents might agree to have you live with your mom during the week and spend time with your dad on the weekends. Any change will be a big **adjustment**, but over time it'll become your new normal way of life.

Some kids spend the school year with one parent and the summer months with the other parent. ⟶

9

# Splitting Time

It's important that you try to spend time with both your parents if they've agreed to share custody. Studies show that children who live with both divorced parents have less **stress** than children who live only with one parent.

You might find it hard to split your time between both parents. Both parents might move to new places. Getting used to living in a new place can be hard. You might have to keep a bag packed to spend time with one parent on the weekends.

Try to keep some special things, such as stuffed animals, at both places to help you feel more comfortable.

11

# Long Distance

No matter where your parents move to, they love you. Of course, it will be hard to deal with parents who live far away from each other. However, that distance doesn't mean their love for you will change. Your mom or dad is just a phone call away.

The parent you spend most of your time with might pay more attention to you than they did before the divorce. This might **annoy** you, but they just want to make sure you're OK.

You might feel more comfortable texting your parent to keep in touch. You can even video chat with them if you're missing them a lot.

13

# Changes for Everyone

A divorce will change things for you and both your parents. One or both might need to get a second job to make ends meet. You might have to go to an after-school program until your parent is done with work.

Helping out at home will make things easier for your parent. It'll also give you a chance to spend more time with them. For example, taking care of your brothers or sisters while your parent makes dinner might give them time to sit down and watch a movie with you later.

Spending time with your parent will let them know you care about their happiness, too. Watching a movie will be a good way for them to unwind. ⟶

# Making Things Worse

Getting divorced won't make all your parents' problems go away. They may continue to argue. Sometimes they might drag you into the middle of things. If they do, you should tell them that this is hurtful not only to your other parent but also to you.

You should be able to talk to your parents about the issues they or you might be having with their divorce. Sometimes finding a time to talk can be hard, but it can help make things better.

It's important that you and your parents find a time to talk if there are issues at home. Ignoring issues will only make them worse.

# How Do You Feel?

Everyone handles their parents' divorce differently. For some kids, divorce might make their life a lot better. For others, a divorce may cause them to feel sad, angry, and confused. It's important that you listen to your feelings and talk to your parents about them.

Sometimes you might not feel comfortable talking to your parents about how you're feeling. Your school **guidance counselor** may also be able to listen to you and help you work through things.

Some kids see a **therapist** to talk about their feelings about their parents' divorce. Going to therapy can be very helpful. ⟶

# New People

After a divorce, it's common for your parent to want to meet new people. They may go on dates and introduce you to these people. You might feel strange about your parent dating and it may take a while for you to get used to it.

It's important that you give the people your parents date a chance. Your parents are trying to find someone who makes them happy. You'll soon realize that these people aren't going to replace your mom or dad.

Hanging out with your dad and his girlfriend might be really fun. Be sure not to judge her too quickly. She could be a wonderful person!

$\longrightarrow$

# Everything Will Be OK

Getting used to your parents being divorced will take time. There will be many changes in your life. You might have to go to a new school. Your parents might fall in love with new people. But everything will be OK. You'll make new friends and you might even come to love your parent's new girlfriend or boyfriend.

Even though your parents aren't married anymore, they both still love you and want what's best for you.

# Glossary

**adjustment:** The act or process of changing to fit new conditions.

**annoy:** To cause someone to feel slightly angry.

**custody:** The right to take care of a child in the eyes of the law.

**guidance counselor:** A person who gives students help making decisions about their education and personal life.

**lawyer:** A person whose job it is to help people in matters relating to the law.

**stress:** Something that causes strong feelings of worry.

**therapist:** A person who helps people deal with mental or emotional problems by talking about those problems.

# Index

**A**

adjustment, 8
after-school program, 14
apartment, 8

**B**

brothers, 8, 14

**C**

custody, 8, 10

**F**

family, 6

**G**

guidance counselor, 18

**H**

habits, 6
houses, 8

**J**

job, 14

**L**

law, 4
lawyer, 8

**M**

marriage, 4

**P**

phone call, 12

**R**

reasons, 4

**S**

school, 8, 14, 22
sisters, 8, 14
stress, 10
summer, 8

**T**

therapist, 18
time, 6, 7, 10, 12, 14, 16, 22

**W**

weekends, 8, 10

# Websites

Due to the changing nature of Internet links, PowerKids Press has developed an online list of websites related to the subject of this book. This site is updated regularly. Please use this link to access the list: www.powerkidslinks.com/help/divorce